BRAINSTORMS

Jennifer Bloom

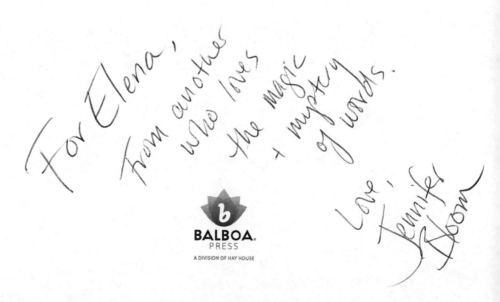

For Elena,
From another
who loves
the magic
+ mystery
of words.

Love,
Jennifer
Bloom

BALBOA
PRESS
A DIVISION OF HAY HOUSE

Interior and Cover Art Credit: Hector Kriete

Balboa Press books may be ordered through booksellers or by contacting:

Balboa Press
A Division of Hay House
1663 Liberty Drive
Bloomington, IN 47403
www.balboapress.com
1 (877) 407-4847

Print information available on the last page.

ISBN: 978-1-5043-6232-0 (sc)
ISBN: 978-1-5043-6234-4 (hc)
ISBN: 978-1-5043-6233-7 (e)

Library of Congress Control Number: 2016911506

Balboa Press rev. date: 11/14/2016

For Big A and Little A,
who teach me every day.

"Look around, look around at how lucky we are
to be alive right now. Look around, look around…"

~ From *Hamilton, An American Musical,* by Lin-Manuel Miranda

TABLE OF CONTENTS

PULL UP A CHAIR

Pull up a chair
and tell me your story,
a friendship we will christen.

For your tale and mine
are intertwined
if we take the time to listen.

THE SPACE BETWEEN

In the space between
you & me
two circles intersect,
and what meets in the middle
is the essence
of our connection.

The space between
you & me
is a playground for our souls,
filled with words
wanting to express
what doesn't need to be said.

In the space between,
we dance together
to an unheard melody
and sing in harmonies
which can be felt
in our hearts.

The space between
you & me
is energy revealing itself,
where my truth
and yours are one
if only for this moment.

A SMILE AND A WINK

With a smile and a wink you touched my heart.
And though our tales seem worlds apart,
When we let our guards down,
We find common ground.
For beyond the outer frame
What makes us human is the same:
    Our heart,
    Our divine spark,
    The still part that knows
What we all really want.

TRESPASSING

I don't belong here.
I'm trespassing in someone else's neighborhood
as I turn off the main road
and onto the quiet, tree-lined streets where people live.

This is where I'll take my walk today
and no one will know the difference.

The woman working in her garden,
the man with the four dogs (two large and two small),
the couple on their power walk,
all smile and wave
a friendly good morning
as though I am a part of the fabric of their world,
as though it would be perfectly natural
if I turned up the next driveway,
walked up to the pale blue house with the red door,
put my key in the lock and stepped inside.

But this is not my home.
I've never walked this path before.

Don't Mistake My Silence for Indifference

Don't mistake my silence for indifference.
I need time to soak things in.
Did you notice the way
The gilded frame around the frosted mirror
Behind the bar reflects more light than the mirror itself?
The way the bartender shakes the drinks
In time to the bluegrass playing on the old record player?
The way the waitress in the long, patterned dress
Disappears and reemerges
Through the half-draped curtain
That blocks the view of a hallway?
I wonder what else is down that hallway.

Don't mistake my silence for indifference.
I'm not the type to wear my heart upon my sleeve.
Have you ever eaten an artichoke from the start?
Taken the time to peel back the thick, outer layers
One by one?
Noticed how each layer is more tender,
More yielding,
More nourishing?
The reward at the center ever more gratifying
Because you took the time to savor the unfolding.

NORDSTROM

I was waiting at the end of a long line
to return something at Nordstrom
when a young woman came up
and said she could help me
at another register.

Relieved that my wait was shortened,
I complimented her coral skirt,
which was light and flirty and made me smile.
It was chiffon with small pleats all around
and short, shorter than what I would wear,
but it suited her petite frame,
bleached blonde bob,
pale porcelain skin,
and the gray t-shirt and black blazer she had paired with it.

As she was processing my return,
a man walked up, another associate.
He had dark hair, almost black,
and skin as pale and flawless as the woman's.
Something struck me about the two of them
as they stood side by side, talking and working.
And then I saw it:
his coral pants, gray shirt, and black blazer.

"You match!" I exclaimed,
"How cool is that!"

They had been working together all day
and hadn't even noticed.

Filling in the Blanks

Studies show that most people,
when looking at a familiar word that is missing a letter,
interpret that missing letter
and don't notice that it's not there.

Most of our universe is empty space
and yet I see
and perceive things to be.
   Solid.
     Liquid.
       Gas.
My mind fills in the blanks.

Is that how it is between you and me,
that we can share an experience
and then go on to tell such different stories about it?
Are we filling in the blanks
with our biases and expectations,
letting our perceptions color our interpretations,
without stepping back to recognize
the lens through which we are judging?

Why is it so hard to notice the missing letters?

Heavy Metal

There once was a man from Frankclay.
In whose head several voices would play.
He'd put up a fight,
From morning 'til night,
To try to tune out what they'd say.

For thirty and seven full years,
Through therapy, pills, shock, and tears.
The voices grew loud,
Had swelled to a crowd,
Giving reason to all of his fears.

Meditation should quiet the mind,
But no moments of silence he'd find.
The man with the voices,
Had run out of choices.
His dilemma was one of a kind.

His doctor said, "I've got a cure!
A remedy known, but obscure.
Implant this device,
With music so nice,
To quell the thoughts you can't endure."

The radio chip in his head,
At first couldn't get him to bed.
Though country sounds nice,
It did not suffice.
He'd try heavy metal instead.

Iron Maiden came on with a roar.
Metallica settled the score.
With Kiss and Black Sabbath,
Judas Priest, Megadeth,
The man heard the voices no more.

SAME HEART

I've heard that cells from the same heart
Beat in time, even when separated
By a hundred miles.

I picture you,
Squinting barefoot at the sea,
Blues and greens reflected in your hopeful eyes.
Your crooked smile almost lost
In a parenthetical embrace
As your bare arms stretch upward
To greet the morning sun.

Do I read your mind
As I lift my morning cup to meet my lips
And remember the time
You told me your truth?
Is it the flutter in your stomach I feel when I wake
From a deep and dreamless sleep,
Unsure of where to begin?

What thread is there that connects your heart to mine?
Wispy strands beyond visible, yet
Bearing some thing
That no earthly fiber could hold.
Because though your heart beats a thousand miles away from mine,
Our feet fall in step as we walk along distant shores.

PRISM

The facet of you that I see
is the person I know you to be.
You seemed clear on the surface,
until sunlight cut through your angles,
distinguishing tones
I hadn't noticed before.

Something within
bends the light,
allowing me to see myself
differently through you.

And I wonder:
When you look at me,
do you see the self that I was
or the person I am becoming?

A Different Version of Me

Perhaps you'd like to see
a different version of me?

Maybe sweet and silly,
flirty and frilly,
strong and stable,
or adept and able?

Could I be fiercely faithful,
totally tasteful,
shockingly shrewd,
or lasciviously lewd?

Am I light as a butterfly
sarcastic and wry,
boisterous and bold,
or quiet and cold?

Which of these might serve me best
if I had to put them to the test?
But then again, who's to say
that I can't be all these things today?

TEQUILA MAKES ME FRISKY, PART 1

It starts with a touch
of the fingertips,
highly charged,
gently stirring,
firing signals of anticipation.

After a moment,
fingers interlace
and fold over one another,
then pull away,
until they are barely touching.

Hands hover,
suspended momentarily by the energy between them,
until they merge once more,
holding tight until one breaks free
and wanders slowly
to wrist, to arm, to elbow
lingering for a moment in the fold,
sending a chill down her side,
before continuing the journey upward
and landing
on shoulder, on collarbone, on neck.

She turns her head to let hand reach jaw,
pulls the thumb into her mouth
then quickly releases it to trace a moist line
from chin to throat to sternum,
through the valley created by her breasts,
finally settling on the soft curve where waist meets hip.

UNCONDITIONAL LOVE

What would it take
    to give myself a break
        from the not good-enoughs,
            the voice inside that scoffs?

What would you need
    to feel fully freed
        from the judgments you make
            on the actions you take?

What would it feel like
    to love our Selves
        unconditionally?

MORNING CUP

Do you fill your cup with coffee?
Or fill it up with tea?
With all your mental anguish,
Or possibility?

Do you pour it out for others
Leaving nothing left for you?
Steeped in good intentions,
The result a bitter brew.

Me, I fill my cup in nature,
With laughter and good friends.
By making time for myself
And a present, mindful lens.

If my cup is filled to brimming,
And teeters on the brink,
There's so much more I have to share
As I offer you a drink.

THE SPACE OF AN EASY MIND

I sit down on the green metal bench.
There must be someplace else I need to be right now,
but I feel like a pause.
And I know I will catch up with the day eventually.

It's quiet,
except for the hum of energy
from the buildings that surround the courtyard,
the crescendo of cars driving by on the road
like swells of ocean waves.
There are birds somewhere.
I can't see them,
but every so often one calls out to its friend
and a conversation is started.
Then silence again.

I'm glad I brought my lunch with me.
Somehow the food tastes better,
   the lettuce more crisp,
      the blueberries more luscious,
         the avocado more sultry,
in this space of an easy mind.

LIFE IN FULL BLOOM

I built a fortress around my heart,
day by day,
year by year,
brick by brick,
until I couldn't feel
what it was like to be me anymore.

Moving through the rhythm of my days,
blocking out the things I thought might wound me,
but also holding in
the fullest expression of myself
for fear of failure,
of rejection.

I am trying to let down my armor,
to let those guards who have been faithfully protecting
the softest, most fragile part of me
take a well-earned break from their duties.

As cracks begin to form
and rays of light penetrate to my core,
I begin to feel more intensely:
the joy of a connection with an unexpected friend,
    and the profound pain when that friend is in
    distress and reaches out for help.
the exquisite ecstasy of allowing myself to really feel love
    and the fear that if I dive too deep I might drown.
the exhilaration of turning a corner
    at the moment the sun dips below the horizon
    and seeing the cloud-streaked sky ablaze with color
    and patterns more magnificent than fireworks,
jolting me awake as I remember.

There is so much more to this life experience
when I allow the emotion to filter through.

The feelings overwhelm me
and I hurry back to the security of my barricade
like a startled turtle hiding in its shell.
But slowly, patiently,
I am building the courage to keep sticking out my neck,
Gentle with myself,
Knowing that one day soon
I will learn to live life in full bloom.

THE EMPTY SHELF

I keep an empty shelf
in the cupboard of my soul,
inviting divine secrets,
synchronistic moments,
and serendipitous encounters.

The empty shelf offers space
for the dream I can't envision,
sparks of inspiration,
a gentle kind of wisdom.

And when that space is filled
I will clear another,
trusting that if I let go,
I will allow more treasures to flow
into the new space that I hold.

I'VE COME TO THE RIVER TO SIT

I've come to the river to sit,
for this is where my soul can breathe,
amidst the grasses and the trees,
watching the clouds above reflected in the water below,
a mirror of myself as I take in this moment.

I've come to the river to sit,
to pause.
And it feels right now
like I am the only thing that is still
in this wild world around me.

I've come to the river to sit.
This is where my soul can grieve.
The movement of the water soothes me,
reminds me that life keeps flowing,
just as the current never changes
its direction.

LIFE CAN BE FUNNY

life can be funny this way:
the way the best and the worst are synchronized
so that the euphoric memory of new life
can rouse a surge of tears
as it is so intertwined with a moment
when the rug was pulled out
from underneath the façade.

life can be funny this way:
the way a person can arrive
during a time of deep despair
and bring in a joy so unexpected
that the wound suddenly doesn't sting with such intensity
and the unknown doesn't feel so frightening.

life can be funny this way:
the way love and rage and fear and gratitude
can circulate through me
as I laugh and cry at the same time.
and the way that comfort comes
not only in the warm embrace of an other
but in the still, cold silence of my self.

life can be funny.

Do I Cry My Eyes to Sleep?

"Do I cry my eyes to sleep?"
asked the boy of himself.

And something in the question
pointed at the girl.
But how can this boy know
the chaos behind
the silky locks
and flirty frocks,
the picture-perfect picket fences of her smile.

"Do I cry my eyes to sleep?"
he asked.
From pain that feels
undeserving
when she compares it
to what could be.

"Do I cry my eyes to sleep?"
he asked.
Not from fright
or to escape the light
but wondering whether
she is worthy or not,
worthy of her lot,
because it seems
like someone forgot
to share it.
And she doesn't know how to care
in a way that makes a real difference.
In a way that will make the little boy turn back
to hand her a tissue
and tell her that it's okay to cry.

WHY DO I FEEL SO SMALL?

Why do I feel so small
when I hear your voice?
With a word or a phrase
I am sent spiraling back in time
and I am a little girl,
meek and timid,
quiet and shy.

No longer the well-spoken woman
the world knows me to be,
my mind is blank
at your questions.
What did you?
Why did you?
Explain to me.
Tell me.

And where once words
may have flowed easily,
and thoughts run free,
the usual chatter inside my head
is suddenly silent
in your presence.

There is nothing.
No words.
No thoughts.
Just silence.
And the feeling of
wanting to curl up
on the window seat
of my childhood room,
nestled against a pillow,
my blanket pulled up to my face.

Waiting for the silence that has filled my head
to switch places with the noise outside
so that I can once again
hear my own voice
instead of yours.

LOST

Clouds closed in.
Fog so thick it seemed easier
To let myself become engulfed
Rather than try to climb
To higher ground.

The peaks seemed farther away
   Each day
      I followed the path
         That led down instead of up.
           Did I have a choice?
           Lost.
             Lost myself.
             I lost myself.
               How does that even happen?
                To stand on my own two feet
              And
              Let
               Myself
               Slip
                Away.

WHAT SHE WANTED

"This is what you wanted!"
screamed letters on a tiny screen.

As if she had a choice.
As if it were a matter
of deciding what to wear
or what flavor of ice cream she preferred.

As if someone had told her when she was small,
"You can choose to be anything you want
When you grow up."

> You can be yourself,
>   or you can be loved.
> You can tell the truth,
>   or you can be included.
> You can speak your mind,
>   or you can be accepted.

As if choice was a luxury,
when all she ever wanted
was not to have to choose.

HEARTBROKEN

This is what a broken heart feels like:

A pressure just behind my sternum
and suddenly I can't breathe.

An ache radiating in all directions
slowly rendering me numb,
as though a steady drip of Lidocaine
was running through my veins.

I want to move.
I want to find something to hold on to,
to pull me back into this moment.
I want to shut down the feeling,
to pretend that it doesn't exist.

But pushing against it only causes it to grow.

SPIRALING

I sit down and feel the energy,
really feel it in my body.
Thousands of spirals swirling
just beneath the surface of my skin.

It is intense.
Not painful, but intense as hell and uncomfortable.
I want to fold,
to protect my heart and my core
even though I know
I am not in danger.

The woman sitting across from me tells me to breathe.
Breathe deeply.
And imagine
my body
making space for the energy,
making space for expansion,
for the spirals to unwind a bit.
"This is not a bad thing," she says.
"You just need to allow it."

That's when the tears start.

Awakening

I almost forgot that world was alive
As I lay in bed and looked at the
Quiet
Still
Life
Outside my picture window.
An old hackberry stands tall.
I can barely see a flutter through its leaves
from inside my sealed container.

I almost forgot the morning music.
Until I stepped outside
to a symphony of sounds
all at once familiar and hard for this city girl to identify.
I recognize the cardinals' call to come for an early breakfast.
Two hummingbirds flit from tree to tree,
sipping water from their leaves, perhaps.
Is that what hummingbirds do?
A lizard scampers across the railing of my deck
and I hear a voice calling from the oak.
Is the squirrel trying to tell me something?
I close my eyes and
listen.
The creek is full today.
I can hear it from my perch
high above the canyon floor.

RISING

We are all reaching toward higher space.
Watch me as I rise in an ever-expanding spiral
like the butterfly that crossed my path
at the bottom of the hill.

She emerged from the tall grass to my left.
I stopped in my tracks and watched
as she passed at the level of my gaze.
She was as high as the treetops
by the time she reached the other side of the street
and continued her journey until
I could see her only as a dark flutter
against a bright blue sky.

Have you ever seen a butterfly hesitate in its upward movement?

Neither have I.

IF HER HEART WERE A FLOWER

If her heart were a flower,
it would never cease to bloom.
Nourished by love from an endless spring,
lilac and rose and aquamarine buds
would sprout each day
on branches that reach
ever skyward
to dance with clouds and rainbows.

"And I can't stop smiling,"
she said, slightly under her breath,
though a stranger walking by might have heard her.

TAPESTRY

Our lives are woven together in moments
     of chance encounters,
     smiles and laughter,
     gestures and touches.

Moments so brief, they seemed like nothing.

But moments add up,
     and moments have meaning,
just as each stitch is an integral part of the whole.

For even if two threads never cross again,
     they will forever be a part of the same tapestry.

Coco Chanel

I can still smell my grandmother's perfume
on one of the sweaters that I kept.
Fourteen years later and I remember
lying on your bed in the mornings
while you drank coffee and juice
and smoked your morning cigarette.

You found the streak in the back of my hair,
a golden shimmer in a sea of brown
that no one else had noticed.
I can find it when the angle is right,
and I feel like a little girl again.

Sometimes I want to pick up the phone,
to call you just to hear your voice
respond to my question:
"What's new, Tia?"
"New York, New Jersey, and New Mexico."
"And don't forget New Haven."

We sat together in the hospital room.
I held your hand as the doctor explained.
I understood your reasons.
Even as I wanted you to hold on,
you knew that the time for healing had passed.

You lay in your bed back home,
and asked me to get you a pound
of chocolate-covered marshmallows,
of fresh bing cherries, and a carton of cigarettes.

"I've done everything I ever wanted to do."
You said those words that echo in my core.
I can still smell my grandmother's perfume,
reminding me that life is not about regrets.

Unraveling

In the beginning,
there was love.
And we saw that it was good.

Our beginning held hope
as our paths entwined,
allowing us to walk
hand in hand
down the road for a time.

With a knot at one end
rooting us,
our strands wound tighter
with each of us reaching further
to try to meet at the other end,
finding that the harder we pulled,
the more unyielding the rope,
as though rigid under the pressure
of its own resistance.

But now,
when I let go,
relax my pull,
the fibers loosen,
edges fray, and the jute
begins to separate from its mate.

The strands become distinct
until it is easy to distinguish
the one from the other.
Like a spring coiled tight
and suddenly released,
the two yarns unravel
with a quickening speed,
ease and fluidity,
revealing that they are each
strong enough
to stand on their own.

CLOSURE

I'm sitting on a wooden pew.
It is nice that someone thought
to put the blue cushion on top.
Who knows how long I will be waiting here.

If I close my eyes, I could be in a church
or in the synagogue in Bombay we visited together
so many years ago.

Instead, the woman beside me
wants to talk about where our kids go to school,
about work, about traffic,
the stuff of every day.

But today is not an every day.
Today is a reminder of a day fourteen years ago
when you rode up on your white horse
to embark on our journey together.
It's a reminder of drumbeats and dancing,
a fusion of family and friends and festivities.
And of all the little moments that brought us to today.

I sit here now,
surrounded by strangers,
and wait for my name to be called,
for the last tie to be severed
by a simple signature,
with no greater ceremony than
getting a driver's license at the DMV.

JASMINE

The scent of jasmine on the trail brings me back
to the window seat in my bedroom on Napoli Drive.
It's funny how nostalgia creeps in
just when I need most to remember.

    Sitting on the front porch with Dad
    and picking strawberries for our homemade ice cream.

    A little boy who brought me a flower
    on the day of our grandpa's funeral.

    Making a waterslide with a garden hose
    and an inflatable pool,
    then sending my sister down to test it.

    Taking batting practice with tennis balls
    and seeing how many we could hit over the roof.

    Putting on shows to the soundtracks
    of *Cats* and *Starlight Express*.

I know it wasn't all the stuff of sitcoms and musicals,
but that's not how my memory works.
The memories smell sweet today,
just like the jasmine.

WALK WITH ME FOR A MOMENT

Walk with me for a moment.
You don't need to leave your whole life behind,
don't need to cancel the plans you've made for next Thursday.
I won't ask you to change your mind,
only to stroll by my side for a time
and share some company
on this journey.

Let me share my secrets
        and I will receive yours.
Let my heart be a soft nest
        in which to cradle your fears,
                your wildest dreams,
                        the swirling stirrings of your imagination.

I will look after them until the time is ripe,
and we both know the time will come
for us to release one another,
without fanfare or tug-of-wars,
without a long and tearful goodbye.
Just a gentle release,
as you veer off to the left and I continue on.

Unwavering.

Even as the small part of me longs to call you back.

Even as I feel a twitch in the high part of my nose
when I remember the day
that we chanced to walk down the same road.

FIVE FOOT ZERO

I remember when he was small
and I used to shoot love into his heart.
"Pshew! Pshew! Pshew!"
I smiled and he laughed
while my index finger gently poked his chest.
He was scared, and I told him
that his name meant "brave."
"What does brave mean, Mama?"
"Brave means being strong when you are scared."

I put a dream catcher in his window
never knowing the faces of the monsters
that haunted his dreams.
He held a Mickey Mouse light saber
to help him fight his battles of the night
with glowing rainbow light.

And now I see in him the boy he was
and the man he is becoming,
equal parts of each grappling for territory
within his expanding frame.
At five foot zero, he fills the bed
as he stretches from corner to corner.
No longer voicing his fears,
my gentle warrior navigates his world
with dignity and compassion.

I stand in the doorway and watch him sleep.
In my mind, I trace a heart over his chest
and take up my anointed arrow
to send a bolt of love across the room.

It lands right on target.

THE MOMENT

It feels as if the energy
is draining out of me,
slowly melting
in a pool by my feet.

Sometimes I want to get off this path
and switch to another,
just take a skip
and be on someone else's journey.

I pause
to listen to the birds
and listen to the water
and listen to the music
dancing in my heart.

I notice the feeling of the warm tea cup in my hand,
the light flavor of silver needle,
the cool, spring air slightly raising the hairs on my arms,
the smell of a cigarette just far enough away,
the sound of a waterfall faintly coming through
the Beethoven that plays in my ear.

I try to pay attention
to the details of the moment.
The way my fingers feel as they stroke the keys,
squiggly lines of green and red
emerging under words that don't come out right
because I am typing as fast as I can think.
There will always be mistakes
when I am typing as fast as I can think.

But I can change the words,
string them together
in a new way
to express the feeling of now,
this moment,
when I am chilled and warmed at the same time.

On the Verge

A painter would notice these things:
The way the water peaks slightly
over rocks beneath the surface.
The way the willows blow in the wind.
The way the birds dart up and down and over the bridge.
The way the light hits the clouds from different angles,
revealing more shades of gray and white than I knew existed.

A painter could capture the muted hues
of yellow and green and brown
in the tall grass along the bank across from where I sit.
The neon green moss that is forming on the
legs of the bridge to the right.
The deep red of the barn
through the thinning foliage.
The steel gray of the metal roof.

A composer might capture the sounds:
Of leaves rustling in the breeze,
of wind chimes playing a spontaneous tune,
the constant flow of the current,
the steady hum of the tractor in the distance.

There are the smells.
The cold green air through my nostrils,
the moisture of a sky about to rain,
coffee spiced with cinnamon, nutmeg, and chili.

But how to express the sense of ease
in this space?
On the verge of a storm,
of movement.
On the edge of land and water,
stability and fluidity.
I don't need to look for shelter yet.
I can find peace in a few light sprinkles.

SHIMMER

Last night the canyon was filled
With fireflies.
I hadn't seen them in almost a year.
I sat and watched their show
As though I was the one for whom they glowed,
As though I could understand their story.

Sometimes little things will pop
Into my head.
They surprise me every time.
A random slice of conversation from so many years ago,
The way the pillows were lined up just so,
The way you looked at me that morning.

I don't know where they come from,
Don't know where they go.
At times I have the urge to
Bottle them into jars and line them up,
An apothecary of memories in my mind.
Or else I want to steep myself in the feeling,
Add them up to make some sort of meaning,
But the thoughts are just too fleeting.
So I sit back and watch them shimmer
And fade.

Tequila Makes Me Frisky, Part 2

The first touch feels electric.
Currents pass between them,
Leaving her arms limp
and energized
at the same time.

She presses forward as
a warm pressure rises in her core,
radiates in all directions.
Pulsing,
moving up
to her heart and throat,
moving down
to her abdomen and pelvis,
expanding, spreading
along her limbs,
all the way down
to her fingertips.

Breathing hard and barely breathing,
savoring each touch and movement
until the force of desire is too strong to hold back.
And she is overcome.
It is not her, and yet it is fully her,
fully present, fully feeling, fully expressing.
Yearning for the release,
even knowing
that the release will bring the end.

Last Kiss

standing silent, neither wanting to say goodbye,
he slowly stretched his hands to hold her face.
they had kissed before, but never like this,
a slow, tender kiss that melted her heart into his.
she reached for him and caught his arms and held them,
dug her fingers into their sides as she tried to hold on
and felt him slipping away at the same time.
and though a part of her wanted to cry, instead she smiled.
because she knew that it was perfect, that life was moving forward
and that the ending could only mean the beginning of something new.

CHANGING THE WORLD

Sometimes it feels
like I pass my days
lost in my head
and a cup of tea.
But secretly,
    quietly,
        magnificently,
I am changing the world.

I Am Afraid to Start

Fearing how the story will end,
I am afraid to start.

Does that ever happen to you?

My mind spins a web of permutations,
Frantic factorizations,
Searching for the right combination,
A Choose Your Own Adventure
That I can't put down
Until I've found the right path,
Only to find that what I was searching for
Wasn't the holy grail at the end of the journey,
But the courage to begin in the first place.

THE WILDFLOWERS ARE STARTING TO SPROUT

The wildflowers are starting to sprout
on the shoulders of highways,
the hills along the side of the road,
my neighbors' yards.
Their seeds will be blown and scattered,
each one holding the potential
of all creation.

Does the flower worry about
which seeds will take root
and which will wash away with the next rain?
Does she hold them close,
not wanting to squander
the precious gifts she holds within her heart?
Or does she release,
with joyful abandon,
surrendering to the mystery of the unknowing?

More and more I remember
that the seed that is blown
from where I stand,
never to be seen again,
may very well land
and grow in someone else's garden.

STANDING ON THE PARTED SHORE

the fear swells,
like a wave
in her chest,
as she stands at the edge of the water.

she knows
that the passage to the other side
is not as long or as deep
as it looks from the surface.

she only needs to take
one
deep
breath
and start.

a moment.

it takes one moment
of courage,
of faith,
and then there is no turning back.

she will be moving.
and the current will carry her.
and the water will cradle her.
and there will be no effort.

and when she emerges
on the other side,
the fear will be gone,
and in its place
will be a world
more beautiful than she can imagine.

it takes one step.
a twitch of the foot
and she will be on her way,
and she will be safe,
and she will be loved.

CHAIN REACTION

Do you try to find order in chaos,
The calm in the eye of the storm?
Do you search for the perfect solution
To a problem that's not yet been formed?

If I stand in a room full of dominoes
And knock over one with my toe,
Should I try to stop the reaction?
Or relax and just let it go?

Each Day

I'm doing the best I can
with each day that I'm living,
to try to embrace the gifts I've been given.

Sometimes I soar.
Sometimes I squeak by.
Sometimes I just want to lie down and cry.

Some days are light;
Others are packed.
I hope I won't let things slip through the cracks.

I aim to be kind
to the people I know
and I'm sorry for any of the hurt I may sow.

One thing I've found
I try not to forget:
The easier I am, the easier life gets.

PREPARING FOR FLIGHT

The geese are preparing for their migration,
teaching the young ones how to fly in formation.
Soon it will be time for them to move on from this place.
But not today.
Today they will stay.
Today they will give their children one more tool
to help them survive.

Even for my flock
today is a day for standing still,
for appreciating the moment,
for teaching and for learning.

I close my eyes to listen to the geese.
And think about the things
I will give to my young
to prepare them for their migration
    so the road bumps and hurdles of life
    will not hinder their flight,
        so they will know when to follow
        and when to take the lead,
            and so the love that surrounds them
            will buoy them on their journey.

Then they will have no choice but to soar.

Metamorphosis

I am a caterpillar growing too big for my skin.
I feed on the world around me,
moving slowly and deliberately,
consuming more than I can hold,
molting to make room for my body,
ever expanding and increasing.

I weave a tapestry around my soul,
burying myself deep inside,
withdrawing,
but never shutting down
the essence of who I am.

I am a butterfly who changes the world.
I draw sweet nectar from the flowers of life,
fueling my soul and allowing my divine spirit
to radiate the vibrant colors and patterns of joy.

I pollinate love and light and truth,
scattering the seeds in all directions,
never knowing where they may land
and what may grow in their presence.

I am earthy and flighty,
camouflaged and colorful,
transformed and transforming,
a never-ending transformation of myself.

IMAGINE THE POSSIBILITY

What a gift that we can begin again.
Imagine the possibilities!
I sit on the deck and listen to the birds
sing their morning song,
slightly different from the day before.
The sun peeks its head above the tops of trees
as the wind rattles their leaves.
And I wonder how many new cells
there are in my body today
and how many have been shed.
Imagine the possibility
of a few hundred new days,
almost the same,
yet slightly different
than the one before.

SAME OLD TUESDAYS

Tuesdays often feel the same.

The morning routine:
pack lunches
make breakfast
hopefully feed myself too.

The drive to school:
twists and turns on a country road
traffic backed up just a bit
where the creek passes under the highway
and I follow the creekside path
only to emerge back into suburbia
where traffic lights, grocery stores, and rows of houses in between
mark my way.

It's a faster drive back,
The traffic is thin on the highway heading north
so I forego the scenic for the efficient.

The events on the calendar:
pre-programmed, pop-up reminders cycle through the day
as though I needed them to remember.
Perhaps a visit to the chiropractor will realign
the time as weeks seem to flow into one another.
The steady stream of routine
comforts an anxious mind.
But today I have the urge to rewind,
look back in time, and I find
That even after all these same old Tuesdays,
Everything is different.

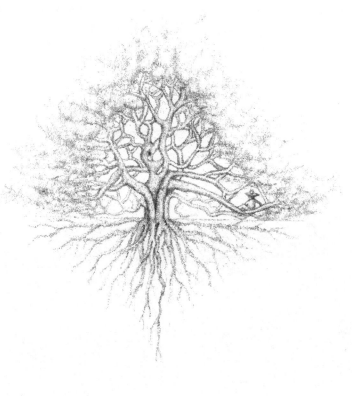

WHAT IF?

What if
the only thing
that mattered right now
was being here
together?

Bliss

It's 7:30 on a Saturday night.
I'm standing in my kitchen
chopping organic veggies
from my farm box.
My son lies on the sofa
in the family room
reading a book.
My baby girl is sleeping
in her bouncy chair.

It is quiet.

For a moment I stop
and notice that I'm smiling.
Not a big tooth-baring smile,
but the smile of pure contentment.

A Piece of Me

She said, "I wanna snuggle up with you, Mama."

I leaned against the headboard as she climbed on me,
curled herself into a ball like a kitten,
and laid her sweet, angel head upon my heart.

I kissed her crown and let my lips linger
in her soft curls.
I bent my head to meet hers and rested it there
until I heard her breathing, long and slow.
Sleeping.

I kissed her again and gently squeezed the tender body
that not too long ago had been a part of mine.
And we lay there as I watched the sky turn to dusk,
knowing that she will always be a piece of me.
And I, her.

ALL OF MY BABIES ARE SLEEPING

All of my babies are sleeping,
And I savor the stillness.
I will put aside the urge to do
One more thing.
The perception of not enough
Time
   Space
      Peace
A distraction from feeling how much
Time
   Space
      Peace
There really is.

So all those things I saved for later can wait
The only thing working in this house tonight
Will be the dishwasher,
Gently humming me to sleep.

SADNESS COMES IN WAVES

Sadness comes in waves,
its triggers unpredictable.
One day the sight of my daughter
laughing with her friends in dance class
sent me over the edge.
Sometimes it's the feel of her hand in my grip,
and the knowing that I will need to release it.

She places her index finger on my nose
and asks me to do the same to her.
Our foreheads touch as we kiss goodnight.
She says she saw someone do that on an airplane once.

There are times when I have the urge
to engulf her and squeeze so tightly,
as though I was pulling her back into my womb.
It takes all my strength to loosen the grip,
giving her room to become herself,
though I would keep her wrapped up in my love forever.

WALKING COMPANION

She surprised me on my walk tonight
for she did not show her face
until I was heading home.

I had resigned myself
to gazing at the stars.

What was it that compelled
me to cross the street
at precisely the moment,
so that when I turned to look
over my left shoulder,
I saw her?

Having just risen over the treetops
she traced the outline
of branches
barely adorned
by blossoms and young leaves.

I caught my breath and watched
her amber glow
rising in a nearly perfect orb,
overwhelmed with awe
that I was blessed
to witness this moment.

I stood anchored to the earth,
even as my soul
seemed to drift
slightly out of my body.
Heavy and light at the same time.

She followed me home,
sometimes hiding
behind the houses and trees
that lined the side of the road.
But I took comfort
knowing that she was beside me,
a faithful companion in the darkness.

Prey

She stopped,
Crouched low,
And fixed her gaze.
Slowly she began to move
With singular intention,
Slinking forward with the stealth of a fox,
Or that of a child who has crept
Out of her room for a midnight treat.

He seemed to sense her,
Though he kept nibbling on his lunch,
Perhaps secretly taunting her to come closer,
Waiting until just the last minute to fly up into the tree.
Still, she darted after him

Only to be halted by an annoying tug at her chest.
The leash had run out of slack.
The leash always runs out of slack and yet,
She always goes after the squirrel.
She just can't help herself.

Offering

Take this offering
from my heart.
No need to pay me back.
The gift is yours
to receive
without strings attached.

Love is what
I have to give.
This much I know is true.
And if my fear
should stifle me,
'twould only punish you.

We all wear masks
to shield ourselves
from being broken down.
But when we open
up our hearts,
connection can be found.

So come, my friend,
and take my hand.
There's no need for confusion.
I'll be me
and you'll be you.
The rest is just illusion.

THE RAINS HAVE PASSED

The rains have passed
and we walk out onto the porch
into the cool, crisp air,
the void after the storm.
I shiver slightly
as the moist air hits my bare arms.
Your body is close to mine.
I can feel your warmth even without us touching,
feel the energy between us,
like two magnets being held
just far enough apart
that an outside force can keep them separate,
even as they yearn to be together.
The touch of your fingertips,
merging with mine,
brings me back to this moment.
I had started to wander
into the clouds.

WHEN THE REST OF THE WORLD FALLS AWAY

When the rest of the world falls away,
we sit side by side in the moonlight.
Tentative.
Perhaps this is too big for both of us.
Perhaps we are both unsure.
Maybe it's just the cool evening breeze.
that nudges us closer together.
Or, perhaps the purpose
that can't be put into words,
is the one which makes the most sense.

REGRET

I wish I would have held you
just a little longer
in the moment when you needed a connection.

I wish I would have held you
just a bit tighter
and allowed my heart to soften.

Instead I let my ego in,
afraid of your rejection.
When perhaps the truth is we both need
a loving ear to listen.

YOU AND ME

hold me and tell me that you love me
without turning to run away.

look into my eyes
and let us melt into one another.

take my hand and squeeze it tight.

smile.

put your hands on my arms
and feel my love radiate to you.

hold my hand once more
as we walk down the road,
uncertain of where we are going
or where we have been,
but knowing so well
that in this moment
there is only you and me.

I Wanted to Tell You a Story

I wanted to tell you a story
as we sat under the tree,
to share a piece of my heart,
a glimpse inside of me.

I mustered up the courage,
dug deep inside my soul,
putting together pieces
to make the picture whole.

I wove humor and sadness,
some moments of madness,
and even a few of my demons to banish.

The highs and the lows,
the peaks and the woes,
until I was utterly stripped to the bone.

You turned and you asked,
"Is that the last
of this tale that you've been spinning?"

I said, "My friend,
there is no end.
We are always just beginning."

THE IN-BETWEEN

I can feel the seasons changing
and I don't like it.
Not this time.

I can feel it in the morning air on my arms
urging me to turn back and grab a jacket.
The chill feels too unfamiliar.
I feel it in the gentle creases on my face that greet me each morning,
the silver sparkles that are sprouting on my head.
They surprise me every day.
I feel it in the picture of my kids by my bed,
frozen on a day several years ago
that I can hardly remember.

The leaves that fall on the road
stir my imagination
of ghosts and goblins and
the circularity of time.
But I'm not ready for hibernation.

This year I want to hold on to the carefree
frolic of summer,
of breezy dresses and flip-flops,
and days that bleed into night
as the sun refuses to close his eyes
even as the moon begins her evening climb.
This year I want to stay in
the in-between.

THE FIELD

Someone is planting seeds all around me.
I lie down in the barren field and close my eyes and count to ten.
Nothing.

I close my eyes again and listen.
The airplane flying overhead.
The gentle sway of distant tree limbs moved by the breeze.
The hiss of air as it streams into my nostrils.

My mind is impatient.
It wants to see the results.
It wants to see the first green sprouts emerge on the landscape,
the first physical evidence of the life that is buried within the soil.

I close my eyes and feel.
The warmth on my face.
The dampness of the Earth slowly seeping
through the clothes on my back.
A mosquito on my toe.
A deep peace coursing through my veins.
And through my closed eyes I finally see
That what is emerging will be magnificent.

REFLECTION

I like the symmetry of this moment
as I sit silent on the same couch,
in the same spot,
wrapped in a blanket,
surrounded by boxes,
filled with a sense of ease.

The last night in this home
is a reflection of the first.
And yet, in that reflection
I view myself in a different light,
as a hand gently gliding
on the surface of a still pond
would allow me to see myself transformed
by the movement of the water.

Do You Ever Wonder?

Do you ever wonder what would have happened
if you had done something else?

If you had opened your heart instead of playing cool,
or held back harsh words that still linger on morning dew?
If you had shifted your eyes to meet a gaze
instead of glancing away a moment too soon?
Or sat a little closer on a late winter's night
instead of turning to face a distant moon?

Do you ever wonder where you would be
if circumstances hadn't intervened
to land us in divergent streams,
floating across a dark and lonely landscape,
wondering if we will make it home again?

We are not so different, you and I.

RETURNING

There is no such thing as too much time gone by
to make a change,
to make a difference,
to reach out to an old friend.

Today I took a new path.
Snowball looked wistfully to left
As I nudged her leash straight on.
She kept looking back at me
As if to ask, "Is this the way?"
But I don't know any more than she does.
And so I wandered
And wondered
Where the road would lead this day,
Whether I had gone astray,
And when I would get to my destination.

But my mental musings were interrupted
By a tug on the leash.
Snowball had stopped to investigate a new bush.
So I paused too and looked up at the sky,
Laced in grays and whites,
And a small patch where the sun,
With curious intention,
Tried to glimpse through the veil.

A flock of birds darted across the scene,
Fifteen or twenty pairs of fluttering wings
Moving with graceful determination.
To whom are they returning?
Will they be greeted with an open heart?

HOME

Nestled in the trees with nothing but green in sight
except the fireflies,
bringing whimsy and light
to my garden each night,
I stretch and watch the sun set
and the moon rise over hills.
There is ease
in the stillness of this
changing of the guard.

I wake up
to the trees outside my window,
to the music of the birds
who share their nest with me.

My kitchen is nourished
by the energy of my hatchlings,
of lunches packed and midnight snacks.
The sofa in the den weathered
by memories of so many snuggles.

We tell each other the best parts of our day,
Sometimes grand, often mundane.
And I imagine what they will remember when they are grown.

I hope they will know
    they are loved and accepted.
I hope they will live
    without fear or shame.
I hope they will realize
    they are unique and common,
        extraordinary and ordinary.

And that I will always be their home.

Hindsight

There will come a time
when we look back on this day
and remember it as the spark that ignited the flame,
the catalyst that set the ball in motion.

There will come a time
when we will look back on a picture
and remember the smiles without the tears,
the outcome without the angst.

There will come a time
when the swirling storm of turmoil
will be edited out of the frame,
leaving only the rainbow that we formed
from fragments of light.

COMPLETION

I've been trying all day
to find the perfect words to convey
the ending to this story,
the period at the end of the sentence,
the chime that signifies completion.

I turn to my usual tricks:
meditation, my journal, a walk in the sticks.
But my head's not in it anymore.
I've already started moving on
to what the next moment will bring.

The deadline at the end of May,
the things I want to do today.
It's hard to stop the flow of life,
the urge to move from one thing to the next
without taking time to rest.

So I will force myself to pause
if only for a moment, because
something inside of me knows
that it is in the space of silence
that new worlds are formed.

There Are No Words

For some things there are no words.

The feeling of hearts connected across time and space,
Of knowing what someone is thinking even without them saying it,
Of picking up the phone to send a message
To find that love is writing at the same time.

When I think about love
In all its forms,
I wish I could describe the rush of energy I felt
When I stood underneath the path
Of hundreds of birds as they migrated up the canyon,
The feeling of wanting to go back in for my camera
And knowing that if I turned my back for a moment
They would be gone.

When I think about loss and pain and heartache and fear
And tears
And tears
And tears I can't explain,
There are no words.

To love is to embrace the risk.
To love is to embrace the risk that one day I will lose love.
One day I will lose love.
There is no question of that.
Children grow.
Loved ones go.
People change.
I am changing every day. And tomorrow

I will look at love through a different lens.
But today I can let myself stand in awe,
Let my body become overwhelmed with the feeling
Contained within this magnificent impermanence
Of love
For which
There are no words.

ACKNOWLEDGMENTS

Brainstorms would not be here in this form without a constellation of supportive people in my life. I would like to thank them for all that they offer me. Several people merit an explicit acknowledgement.

Hector Kriete created all of the artwork that is in this book. I am grateful for his artistic vision, for the friendship that formed as a result of this creative endeavor, and for the time we spend on the trail.

I wrote my first poem in January 2014 and sent it in an email to Jennifer Hritz. Thus she became my first audience. She has read every poem I've ever written, including several drafts of this collection. She provided critical feedback on early drafts and edited the final manuscript. She is a provocative and talented novelist, and her dedication to her craft has inspired me for many years. I am eternally grateful for her support and friendship.

We all need people to coax us a little past our comfort zone. Phillip Estes dared me to publicly share my poetry on Facebook in a 30-day poetry month challenge. The bravery and honesty in his poetry motivates me to write from the heart. Thank you for inspiration and for being a sounding board when I have been stuck.

When I was a little girl and people asked me what I wanted to be when I grew up, my list was long and varied: doctor, singer, writer, fashion designer, caterer, event planner... I thank my parents, Myrna and Steve Greenberg, for never telling me I had to choose one thing. They taught me that anything is possible, that it is never too late to follow a passion, and that kindness and generosity of spirit are two of the most important attributes a person can cultivate.

Thank you to my sister, Melanie Greenberg, for egging me on, for being the smartest, funniest, wittiest gal I know, and for reading and editing this collection at many points along the way.

Thank you to Alva Greenberg, George Gonzalez, Lindy Kummings, Jamil Thomas, and Kristen Skoglund. They each read an early draft of this collection and provided feedback and encouragement.

Thank you to Karol Kaye Harris for inviting me to see myself through an expanded lens and for the conversations that lift my vision. Thank you to Wendy Betron for always making me smile; to Katherine Torrini for her creative coaching; to Eric Pacheco and Justin Jagoda for each working with me to transform poetry into song; to Sharmila Advani, Martha Feferman, Devanshi Patel, Shelly Sethi, and Nayana Shahane for being excellent cheerleaders; and to Leslie Shaffer and Diana Berrent because I love you.

Inspiration comes to me from many sources: insights from science, the beautiful sky and Earth and all its creatures, conversations with strangers, my children, and memories of my own childhood. I appreciate all of the people in my life who have inspired me through our conversations and shared experiences. You have broadened my perspective, allowed me to find meaning in the mundane, and offered me a better understanding of the myriad ways in which love can manifest. I trust that you know who you are.

Finally, to my kiddos: thank you for being willing to play along with all my notions, for trusting me, and for opening my eyes to see the world through yours. I am honored to be your mom.

"Five Foot Zero" was originally published in the Winter 2015 issue of *Brain.Child* Magazine (Volume 20, Issue 1).

About the Author

Jennifer Bloom is a poet, singer, scholar, and mother. She holds a B.A. in English from Yale University and a Masters of Science in Health and Social Behavior from the Harvard School of Public Health. A native of Southern California, she now lives in Austin, TX with her two children and their dog, Snowball. She never intended to write poetry; she just needed to write. What started as a journaling exercise has transformed into a re-imagining of herself and her relationship to the world around her. Experience more at Jennifer-Bloom.com.

Made in the USA
Middletown, DE
03 January 2017